# SOCIAL LIFE IN OLD VIRGINIA
## BEFORE THE WAR

"*Tall lilies, white as angels' wings and stately as the maidens that walked among them.*"

# Social Life in Old Virginia

*Before the War*

BY

THOMAS NELSON PAGE, 1853-1922.

*With Illustrations by*

THE MISSES COWLES

 BOOKS FOR LIBRARIES PRESS
FREEPORT, NEW YORK

First Published 1897
Reprinted 1970

INTERNATIONAL STANDARD BOOK NUMBER:
0-8369-5533-1

LIBRARY OF CONGRESS CATALOG CARD NUMBER:
73-130560

# List of Illustrations

vii

# List of Illustrations

# Introduction

*Which none need read unless he pleases.*

NO one can be more fully aware of the shortcomings of this brief sketch of Social Life in the South before the War than is the writer. Its slightness might readily have excused it from republication. And yet it has seemed well to let it go forth on its own account, to take such place as it may in the great world of books. One reason is the partiality of a few friends who have desired to see it in this form. Another is the absolute ignorance of the outside world of the real life of the South in old times, and the desire to correct the picture for the benefit of the younger generation of Southerners themselves. One of the factors in that life was slavery. The most renowned picture of Southern life is one of it as it related exclusively to that institution. As an argument in the case then at bar, it was one of the most powerful ever penned. Mrs. Stowe did more to free the slave than all the politicians. And yet her picture is not one which any Southerner would willingly have stand as a final portrait of Southern life. No one could understand that life who did not see it in its entirety.

The old life at the South passed away in the flame of war and in the yet more fiery ordeal of Reconstruction. So complete was this devastation that now unless one knows where to go he may search in vain for its reality. Its remnants lie scattered in far-off neighborhoods ; its fragments almost overgrown with the tangles of a new life. The picture of it which at present is mainly presented is wholly

# Introduction

unreal. The Drama is one of the accepted modes of judging of passing life. It is assumed to be a reasonably true reflection of the life it pretends to portray. If this standard shall be accepted, what a life that must have been which existed in the South! The bloodhounds, brute and human, that chased delicate women for sport, have mainly been given up. But their place has been taken by a different species of barbarian if possible even more unreal than those they supplanted. Quite a large crop of so-called Southern plays, or at least plays in which Southerners have figured, has of late been introduced on the stage, and the supposititious Southerner is as absurd a creation as the wit of ignorance ever devised. The Southern girl is usually an underbred little provincial, whose chief characteristic is to say " reckon " and " real," with strong emphasis, in every other sentence. And the Southern gentleman is a sloven whose linen has never known starch; who clips the endings of his words; says "Sah" at the end of every sentence, and never uses an "r" except in the last syllable of "nigger." With a slouched hat, a slovenly dress, a plentiful supply of "sahs," and a slurred speech exclusively applied to "niggers," he is equipped for the stage. And yet it is not unkindly meant: only patronizingly, which is worse. That Thackeray, Matthew Arnold, Lawrence, and other visitors whose English passes current, declared after a visit to America that they found the purest English speech spoken in Virginia, goes for nothing.

If the writers of the plays referred to would attend one of the formal assemblies under one of the old social associations in the South, — for instance,

# Introduction

the St. Cecilia Ball in Charleston, one of the final refuges of old-fashioned gentility and distinguished manners, — they would get some idea of what old-time good breeding and high courtesy were.

It is perhaps partly to correct this erroneous idea of the Old South that this little essay has been attempted. But mainly it has been from sheer affection.

T. N. P.

# SOCIAL LIFE IN OLD VIRGINIA BEFORE THE WAR

LET me see if I can describe an old Virginia home recalled from a memory stamped with it when a virgin page. It may, perhaps, be idealized by the haze of time; but it will be as I now remember it.

The mansion was a plain " weather-board " house, one story and a half above the half-basement ground floor, set on a hill in a grove of primeval oaks and hickories filled in with ash, maples, and feathery-leafed locusts without number. It was built of timber cut by the " servants " (they were never termed slaves except in legal documents) out of the virgin forest, not long after the Revolution, when that branch of the family moved from Yorktown. It had quaint dormer windows, with small

panes, poking out from its sloping up-
stairs rooms, and long porches to shelter
its walls from the sun and allow house
life in the open air.

A number of magnificent oaks and
hickories (there had originally been a
dozen of the former, and the place from
them took its name, " Oakland "), under
which Totapottamoi children may have
played, spread their long arms about it,
sheltering nearly a half-acre apiece;
whilst in among them and all around
were ash and maples, an evergreen or
two, lilacs and syringas and roses, and
locusts of every age and size, which in
springtime filled the air with honeyed
perfume, and lulled with the " murmur
of innumerable bees."

There was an " office " in the yard;
another house where the boys used to
stay, and the right to sleep in which was
as eagerly looked forward to and as
highly prized as was by the youth of
Rome the wearing of the *toga virilis*.
There the guns were kept; there the

*The Plantation House.*

dogs might sleep with their masters, under, or in cold weather even on, the beds; and there charming bits of masculine gossip were retailed by the older young gentlemen, and delicious tales of early wickedness related, all the more delightful because they were veiled in chaste language phrased not merely to meet the doctrine, *maxima reverentia pueris debetur*, but to meet the higher truth that no gentleman would use foul language.

Off to one side was the orchard, in springtime a bower of pink and snow, and always making a pleasant spot in the landscape; beyond which peeped the ample barns and stables, and farther yet lay the wide green fields.

Some of the fields that stretched around were poor, and in places where the rains had washed off the soil, red "galls" showed through; but the tillage was careful and systematic, and around the house were rich hay-fields where the cattle stood knee-deep in clover.

# Social Life

The brown worm fences ran in lateral lines, and the ditches were kept clean except for useful willows.

The furniture was old-timey and plain, — mahogany and rosewood bed-steads and dressers black with age, and polished till they shone like mirrors,

*" There the guns were kept."*

hung with draperies white as snow;
straight-backed chairs generations old
interspersed with common
new ones; long sofas
with claw feet; old

*" Bookcases filled with brown-backed,
much-read books."*

shining tables with slender brass-tipped
legs, straight or fluted, holding some
fine old books, and in springtime a blue

or flowered bowl or two with glorious roses; bookcases filled with brown-backed, much-read books. This was all.

The servants' houses, smoke-house, wash-house, and carpenter-shop were set around the " back yard," with " mammy's house " a little nicer than the others; and farther off, upon and beyond the quarters hill, " the quarters," — whitewashed, substantial buildings, each for a family, with chicken-houses hard by, and with yards closed in by split palings, filled with fruit trees, which somehow bore cherries, peaches, and apples in a mysterious profusion even when the orchard failed.

Beyond the yard were gardens. There were two, — the vegetable garden and the flower garden. The former was the test of the mistress's power; for at the most critical times she took the best hands on the place to work it. The latter was the proof of her taste. It was a strange affair : pyrocanthus hedged it on the outside; honeysuckle ran riot

over its palings, perfuming the air;
yellow cowslips in well-regulated tufts
edged some borders, while sweet peas,
pinks, and violets spread out recklessly
over others; jonquilles yellow as gold,
and, once planted, blooming every spring
as certainly as the trees budded or the
birds nested, grew in thick bunches; and
here and there were tall lilies, white as
angels' wings and stately as the maidens
that walked among them; big snowball
bushes blooming with snow, lilacs pur-
ple and white and sweet in the spring,
and always with birds' nests in them
with the bluest of eggs; and in places
rosebushes, and tall hollyhock stems
filled with rich rosettes of every hue and
shade, made a delicious tangle. In the
autumn rich dahlias and pungent-odored
chrysanthemums ended the sweet pro-
cession and closed the season.

But the flower of all others was the
rose. There were roses everywhere;
clambering roses over the porches and
windows, sending their fragrance into

the rooms; roses beside the walks; roses around the yard and in the garden; roses of every hue and delicate refinement of perfume; rich yellow roses thick on their briery bushes, coming almost with the dandelions and buttercups, before any others dared face the April showers to learn if March had truly gone, sweet as if they had come from Paradise to be worn upon young maidens' bosoms, as they might well have done — who knows? — followed by the Giant of Battles on their stout stems, glorious enough to have been the worthy badge of victorious Lancastrian kings; white Yorks, hardly less royal; cloth-of-golds; dainty teas; rich damasks; old sweet hundred-leafs sifting down their petals on the grass, and always filling with two the place where one had fallen. These and many more whose names have faded made the air fragrant, whilst the catbirds and mocking-birds fluttered and sang among them, and the robins foraged in the grass for their greedy yellow-throats waiting in the hidden nests.

Looking out over the fields was a scene not to be forgotten.

Let me give it in the words of one who knew and loved Virginia well, and was her best interpreter : [1] —

"A scene not of enchantment, though contrast often made it seem so, met the eye. Wide, very wide fields of waving grain, billowy seas of green or gold as the season chanced to be, over which the scudding shadows chased and played, gladdened the heart with

[1] Dr. George W. Bagby. His "Old Virginia Gentleman" is perhaps the best sketch yet written in the South. To it I am doubtless indebted for much in this paper. His description might do for a picture of Staunton Hill resting in delicious calm on its eminence above the Staunton River.

*Tobacco.*

wealth far spread. Upon lowlands level as the floor the plumed and tasselled corn stood tall and dense, rank behind rank in military alignment — a serried army lush and strong. The rich, dark soil of the gently swelling knolls could scarcely be seen under the broad lapping leaves of the mottled tobacco. The hills were carpeted with clover. Beneath the tree-clumps fat cattle chewed the cud, or peaceful sheep reposed, grateful for the shade. In the midst of this plenty, half hidden in foliage, over which the graceful shafts of the Lombard poplar towered, with its bounteous garden and its orchards heavy with fruit near at hand, peered the old mansion, white, or dusky red, or mellow gray by the storm and shine of years.

"Seen by the tired horseman halting at the woodland's edge, this picture, steeped in the intense quivering summer moonlight, filled the soul with unspeakable emotions of beauty, tenderness, peace, home.

"How calm could we rest
In that bosom of shade with the friends we
love best!

# Social Life

"Sorrows and care were there —
where do they not penetrate? But,
oh! dear God, one day in those sweet,
tranquil homes outweighed a fevered
lifetime in the gayest cities of the globe.
Tell me nothing; I undervalue naught
that man's heart delights in. I dearly
love operas and great pageants; but I
do know — as I know nothing else —
that the first years of human life, and
the last, yea, if it be possible, all the
years, should be passed in the country.
The towns may do for a day, a week,
a month at most; but Nature, Mother
Nature, pure and clean, is for all time,
— yes, for eternity itself."

The life about the place was amaz-
ing. There were the busy children
playing in groups, the boys of the family mingling with the little darkies as
freely as any other young animals, and
forming the associations which tempered slavery and made the relation one
not to be understood save by those who
saw it. There they were, stooping

*A Typical " Mammy."*

down and jumping up; turning and twisting, their heads close together, like chickens over an "invisible repast," their active bodies always in motion: busy over their little matters with that ceaseless energy of boyhood which could move the world could it but be concentrated and conserved. They were all over the place; in the orchard robbing birds' nests, getting into wild excitement over catbirds, which they ruthlessly murdered because they "called snakes"; in spring and summer fishing or "washing" in the creek, riding the plough-horses to and from the fields, running the calves and colts, and being as mischievous as the young mules they chased.

There were the little girls in their great sunbonnets, often sewed on to preserve the wonderful peach-blossom complexions, with their small female companions playing about the yard or garden, running with and wishing they were boys, and getting half scoldings

from mammy for being tomboys and tearing their aprons and dresses. There, in the shade, near her "house," was the mammy with her assistants, her little charge in her arms, sleeping in her ample lap, or toddling about her, with broken, half-formed phrases, better understood than framed. There passed young negro girls, blue-habited, running about bearing messages; or older women moving at a statelier pace, doing with deliberation the little tasks which were their "work;" whilst about the office or smoke-house or dairy or

wood-pile there was always some movement and life. The peace of it all was only emphasized by the sounds that broke upon it : the call of ploughers to their teams; the shrill shouts of children; the chant of women over their work, and as a bass the recurrent hum of spinning-wheels, like the drone of some great insect, sounding from cabins where the turbaned spinners spun their fleecy rolls for the looms which were clacking in the loom-rooms making homespun for the plantation.

From the back yard and quarters the

laughter of women and the shrill, joyous voices of children came. Far off, in the fields, the white-shirted "ploughers" followed singing their slow teams in the fresh furrows, wagons rattled, and ox-carts crawled along, or gangs of hands in lines performed their work in the corn or tobacco fields, loud shouts and peals of laughter, mellowed by the distance, floating up from time to time, telling that the heart was light and the toil not too heavy.

At special times there was special activity : at ice-getting time, at corn-thinning time, at fodder-pulling time, at threshing-wheat time, but above all at corn-shucking time, at hog-killing time, and at " harvest." Harvest was spoken of as a season. It was a festival. The severest toil of the year was a frolic. Every " hand " was eager for it. It was the test of the men's prowess and the women's skill. For it took a man to swing his cradle through the long June days and keep pace with the bare-necked,

"The test of the men's prowess."

knotted-armed leader as he strode and
swung his ringing cradle through the
heavy wheat.  So it demanded a strong
back and nimble fingers in the binding
to " keep up " and bind the sheaves.
The young men looked forward to it
as young bucks look to the war-path.
How gay they seemed, moving in oblique
lines around the " great parallelograms,"
sweeping down the yellow grain, and,
as they neared the starting-point, chant-
ing with mellow voices the harvest song
"Cool Water"!  How musical was the
cadence as, taking time to get their wind,
they whet in unison their ringing blades !

Though the plantations were large,
so large that one master could not
hear his neighbor's dog bark, there was
never any loneliness : it was movement
and life without bustle ; whilst somehow,
in the midst of it all, the house seemed
to sit enthroned in perpetual tranquillity,
with outstretched wings under its spread-
ing oaks, sheltering its children like a
great gray dove.

Even at night there was stirring
about : the ring of an axe, the infectious music of the banjos, the laughter
of dancers, the festive noise and merriment of the cabin, the distant, mellowed
shouts of 'coon or 'possum hunters, or
the dirge-like chant of some serious
and timid wayfarer passing along the
paths over the hills or through the
woods, and solacing his lonely walk
with religious song.

Such was the outward scene. What
was there within ? That which has
been much misunderstood, — that which
was like the roses, wasteful beyond
measure in its unheeded growth and
blowing, but sweet beyond measure,
too, and filling with its fragrance not
only the region round about, but sending it out unmeasuredly on every breeze
that wandered by.

The life within was of its own kind.
There were the master and the mistress: the old master and old mistress,
the young masters and young mistresses,

32

and the children; besides some aunts and cousins, and the relations or friends

*The Exclusive Property of the Mistress.*

who did not live there, but were only always on visits.

Properly, the mistress should be mentioned first, as she was the most important personage about the home, the presence which pervaded the mansion, the centre of all that life, the queen of that realm; the master willingly and proudly yielding her entire management of all household matters and simply carrying out her directions, confining his ownership within the curtilage solely to his old " secretary," which on the mistress's part was as sacred from her touch as her bonnet was from his. There were kept mysterious folded papers, and equally mysterious parcels, frequently brown with the stain of dust and age. Had the papers been the lost sibylline leaves instead of old receipts and bills, and had the parcels contained diamonds instead of long-dried melon-seed or old flints, now out of date but once ready to serve a useful purpose, they could not have been more sacredly guarded by the mistress. The master usually had to hunt for a long period for any particular paper, whilst the mistress could in a half-hour have arranged everything in perfect order; but the chaos was regarded by her with veneration as real as that with which she regarded the mystery of the heavenly bodies.

On the other hand, outside of this piece of furniture there was nothing in the house of which the master even pretended to know. It was all in her keeping. Whatever he wanted he called for, and she produced it with a certainty and promptness which struck him as a perpetual miracle. Her system appeared to him as the result of a wisdom as profound as that which fixed and held the firmament. He would not have dared to interfere, not because he was afraid, but because he recognized her superiority. It would no more have occurred to him to make a suggestion about the management of the house than about that of one of his neighbors; simply because he knew her and acknowledged her infallibility. She was, indeed, a surprising creature — often delicate in frame, and of a nervous organization so sensitive as perhaps to be a great sufferer; but her force and character pervaded and directed everything, as unseen yet as unmistakably as the power of gravity controls the particles that constitute the earth.

It has been assumed by the outside world that our people lived a life of idleness and ease, a kind of " hammock-swung," " sherbet-sipping " existence, fanned by slaves, and, in their pride, served on bended knees. No conception could be further from the truth. The ease of the master of a big plantation was about that of the head of any great establishment where numbers of operatives are employed, and to the management of which are added the responsibilities of the care and complete mastership of the liberty of his operatives and their families. His work was generally sufficiently systematized to admit of enough personal independence to enable him to participate in the duties of hospitality; but any master who had a successfully

conducted plantation was sure to have
given it his personal supervision with an
unremitting attention which would not
have failed to secure success in any other
calling. If this was true of the master,
it was much more so of the mistress.
The master might, by having a good
overseer and reliable headmen, shift a
portion of the burden from his shoul-
ders; the mistress had no such means of
relief. She was the necessary and in-
variable functionary; the keystone of
the domestic economy which bound all
the rest of the structure and gave it its
strength and beauty. From early morn
till morn again the most important and
delicate concerns of the plantation were
her charge and care. She gave out
and directed all the work of the
women. From superintending the set-
ting of the turkeys to fighting a
pestilence, there was nothing which
was not her work. She was mistress,
manager, doctor, nurse, counsellor,
seamstress, teacher, housekeeper, slave,

all at once. She was at the beck and call of every one, especially of her husband, to whom she was "guide, philosopher, and friend."

One of them, being told of a broken gate by her husband, said, " Well, my dear, if I could sew it with my needle and thread, I would mend it for you."

What she was, only her husband divined, and even he stood before her in dumb, half-amazed admiration, as he might before the inscrutable vision of a superior being. What she really was, was known only to God. Her life was one long act of devotion, — devotion to God, devotion to her husband, devotion to her children, devotion to her servants, to her friends, to the poor, to humanity. Nothing happened within the range of her knowledge that her sympathy did not reach and her charity and wisdom did not ameliorate. She was the head and front of the church ; an unmitred bishop *in partibus*, more effectual than the vestry or deacons, more earnest than the rector; she managed her family, regulated her servants, fed the poor, nursed the sick, consoled the bereaved. Who knew of the visits she paid to the cabins of her sick and suffering servants! often, at the dead of night, " slipping down " the last thing to see that her directions were carried out; with her own hands administering medicines or food; ever by her cheeriness inspiring new hope, by her strength giving courage, by her presence awaking faith; telling in her soft voice to dying ears the story of the suffering Saviour; with her hope soothing the troubled spirit, and lighting with her own faith the path down into the valley of the dark shadow. What poor person was there, however inaccessible the cabin, that was sick or destitute and knew not her charity! Who that was bereaved that had not her sympathy!

The training of her children was her work. She watched over them,

inspired them, led them, governed
them; her will impelled them; her
word to them, as to her servants,
was law. She reaped the reward.
If she admired them, she was too
wise to let them know it; but her
sympathy and tenderness were theirs
always, and they worshipped her.

There was something in seeing the
master and mistress obeyed by the plantation and looked up to by the neighborhood which inspired the children with
a reverence akin to awe which is not
known at this present time. It was
not till the young people were grown
that this reverence lost the awe and
became based only upon affection and
admiration. Then, for the first time,
they dared to jest with her; then, for
the first time, they took in that she
had been like them once, young and
gay and pleasure-loving, with coquet-
ries and maidenly ways, with lovers
suing for her; and that she still took
pleasure in the recollection, — this gen-

tle, classic, serious mother among her tall sons and radiant daughters. How she blushed as they laughed at her and teased her to tell of her conquests, her confusion making her look younger and prettier than they remembered her, and opening their eyes to the truth of what their father had told them so often, that not one of them could be as beautiful as she.

She became timid and dependent as they grew up and she found them adorned with new fashions and ways which she did not know; she gave herself up to their guidance with an appealing kind of diffidence; was tremulous over her ignorance of the novel fashions which made them so charming. Yet, when the exactions of her position came upon her, she calmly took the lead, and, by her instinctive dignity, her wisdom, and her force, eclipsed them all as naturally as the full moon in heaven dims the stars.

Such in part was the mistress. As

to the master himself, it is hard to
generalize. Yet there were indeed
certain generic characteristics, whether
he was grave and severe, or jovial and
easy. There was the foundation of a
certain pride based on self-respect and
consciousness of power. There were
nearly always the firm mouth with its
strong lines, the calm, placid, direct
gaze, the quiet speech of one who is
accustomed to command and have his
command obeyed ; there was a contem-
plative expression due to much commun-
ing alone, with weighty responsibilities
resting upon him ; there was absolute
self-confidence, and often a look caused
by tenacity of opinion. There was not
a doubtful line in the face nor a doubtful tone in the voice ; his opinions were
convictions ; he was a partisan to the
backbone ; and not infrequently he was
incapable of seeing more than one side.
This prevented breadth, but gave force.
He was proud, but rarely haughty except
to dishonor. To that he was inexo-

rable. He believed in God, he believed
in his wife, he believed in his blood.
He was chivalrous, he was generous,
he was usually incapable of fear or of
meanness. To be a Virginia gentleman was the first duty; it embraced
being a Christian and all the virtues.
He lived as one; he left it as a heri-
tage to his children. He was fully
appreciative of both the honors and the
responsibilities of his position. He believed in a democracy, but understood
that the absence of a titled aristocracy
had to be supplied by a class more
virtuous than he believed any aristocracy to be. He purposed in his own
person to prove that this was practi-
cable. He established the fact that it
was. This and other responsibilities
made him grave. He had inherited
gravity from his father and grandfather.
The latter had been a performer in the
greatest work of modern times, with
the shadow of the scaffold over him if
he failed. The former had faced the

weighty problems of the new government, with many unsolved questions ever to answer. He himself faced problems not less grave. The greatness of the past, the time when Virginia had been the mighty power of the New World, loomed ever above him. It increased his natural conservatism. He saw the change that was steadily creeping on. The conditions that had given his class their power and prestige had altered. The fields were worked down, and agriculture that had made his class rich no longer paid. The cloud was already gathering in the horizon; the shadow already was stretching towards him. He could foresee the danger that threatened Virginia. A peril ever sat beside his door. He was "holding the wolf by the ears." Outside influences hostile to his interest were being brought to bear. Any movement must work him injury. He sought the only refuge that appeared. He fell back behind the Constitution that his fathers had helped to establish, and became a strict constructionist for Virginia and his rights. These things made him grave. He reflected much. Out on the long verandas in the dusk of the summer nights, with his wide fields stretching away into the gloom, and " the woods " bounding the horizon, his thoughts dwelt upon serious things; he pondered causes and consequences; he resolved everything to prime principles. He communed with the Creator and his first work, Nature.

This communion made him a wonderful talker. He discoursed of philosophy, politics, and religion. He read much, generally on these subjects, and read only the best. His bookcases held the masters (in mellow Elzevirs and Lintots) who had been his father's friends, and with whom he associated and communed more intimately than with his neighbors. Homer, Horace, Virgil, Ovid, Shakespeare, Milton, Dryden, Goldsmith, " Mr. Pope," were his

poets ; Plutarch, Bacon, Burke, and
Dr. Johnson were his philosophers.
He knew their teachings and tried to
pattern himself on them. These "new
fellows" that his sons raved over he
held in so much contempt that his mere
statement of their inferiority was to his
mind an all-convincing argument.

In religion he was as orthodox as
the parson. He might not be a pro-
fessing member of the church; but
he was one of its pillars : ready to
stand by, and, if need were, to fight to
the death for the Thirty-nine Articles,
or the Confession of Faith. Yet,
if he was generally grave, he was
at times, among his intimates and
guests, jovial, even gay. On festive
occasions no one surpassed him in
cheeriness. To a stranger he was
always a host, to a lady always a
courtier. When the house was full of
guests, he was the life of the company.
He led the prettiest girl out for the
dance. At Christmas he took her

*" His thoughts dwelt upon serious things."*

under the mistletoe, and paid her gracious compliments which made her blush and courtesy with dimpling face and dancing eyes. But whatever was his mood, whatever his surroundings, he was always the exponent of that grave and knightly courtesy which under all conditions has become associated with the title " Virginia gentleman."

Whether or not the sons were, as young men, peculiarly admirable may be a question. They possessed the faults and the virtues of young men of their kind and condition. They were given to self-indulgence ; they were not broad in their limitations ; they were apt to contemn what did not accord with their own established views (for their views were established before their mustaches) ; they were wasteful of time and energies beyond belief ; they were addicted to the pursuit of pleasure. They exhibited the customary failings of their kind in a society of an aristocratic character.

But they possessed in full measure the corresponding virtues. They were brave, they were generous, they were high-spirited. Indulgence in pleasure did not destroy them. It was the young French noblesse who affected to eschew exertion even to the point of having themselves borne on litters on their boar-hunts, and who yet, with a hundred pounds of iron buckled on their frames, charged like furies at Fontenoy. So these same languid, philandering young gentlemen, when the crucial occasion came, suddenly appeared as the most dashing and indomitable soldiery of modern times. It was the Norfolk company known as the " Dandies " that was extirpated in a single day.

But, whatever may be thought of the sons, there can be no question as to the daughters. They were like the mother; made in her own image. They filled a peculiar place in the civilization; the key was set to them. They held by a universal consent the first place in the system, all social life revolving around them. So generally did the life shape itself about the young girl that it was almost as if a bit of the age of chivalry had been blown down the centuries and lodged in the old State. She instinctively adapted herself to it. In fact, she was made for it. She was gently bred : her people for generations (since they had come to Virginia) were gentlefolk. They were so well satisfied that they had been the same in the mother country that they had never taken the trouble to investigate it. She was the incontestable proof of their gentility. In right of her blood (the beautiful Saxon, tempered by the influences of the genial Southern clime), she was exquisite, fine, beautiful; a creature of peach-blossom and snow ; languid, delicate, saucy ; now imperious, now melting, always bewitching. She was not versed in the ways of the world, but she had no need to be ; she was better than

that; she was well bred. She had not
to learn to be a lady, because she was
born one. Generations had given her
that by heredity. She grew up apart
from the great world. But ignorance
of the world did not make her provincial. Her instinct was an infallible
guide. When a child she had in her
sunbonnet and apron met the visitors at
the front steps and entertained them in
the parlor until her mother was ready
to appear. Thus she had grown up to
the duties of hostess. Her manners
were as perfectly formed as her mother's,
with perhaps a shade more self-posses-
sion. Her beauty was a title which
gave her a graciousness that well be-
fitted her. She never " came out,"
because she had never been " in ; " and
the line between girlhood and young-
ladyhood was never known. She began
to have beaux certainly before she
reached the line ; but it did her no
harm : she would herself long walk
" fancy free." A protracted devotion

was required of her lovers, and they began early. They were willing to serve long, for she was a prize worth the service. Her beauty, though it was often dazzling, was not her chief attraction.

*An Old Virginia Sideboard.*

That was herself: that indefinable charm; the result of many attractions, in combination and perfect harmony, which made her herself. She was delicate, she was dainty, she was sweet. She lived in an atmosphere created for her, —

the pure, clean, sweet atmosphere of her country home. She made its sunshine. She was generally a coquette, often an outrageous flirt. It did not imply heartlessness. It was said that the worst flirts made the most devoted wives. It was simply an instinct, an inheritance; it was in the life. Her heart was tender towards every living thing but her lovers; even to them it was soft in every way but one. Had they had a finger-ache, she would have sympathized with them. But in the matter of love she was inexorable, remorseless. She played upon every chord of the heart. Perhaps it was because, when she gave up, the surrender was to be absolute. From the moment of marriage she was the worshipper. Truly she was a strange being. In her muslin and lawn; with her delicious, low, slow, musical speech; accustomed to be waited on at every turn, with servants to do her every bidding; unhabituated often even to putting on her dainty slippers or combing her soft hair, — she possessed a reserve force which was astounding. She was accustomed to have her wishes obeyed as commands. It did not make her imperious; it simply gave her the habit of control. At marriage she was prepared to assume the duties of mistress of her establishment, whether it were great or small.

Thus, when the time came, the class at the South which had been deemed the most supine suddenly appeared as the most efficient and the most indomitable. The courage which the men displayed in battle was wonderful; but it was nothing to what the Southern women exemplified at home. There was, perhaps, not a doubtful woman within the limits of the Confederacy. Whilst their lovers and husbands fought in the field, they performed the harder part of waiting at home. With more than a soldier's courage they bore more than a soldier's hardship. For four long years they listened to the noise of the guns, awaiting with blanched faces but undaunted hearts the news of battle after battle ; buried their beloved dead with tears, and still amid their tears encouraged the survivors to fight on. It was a force which has not been duly estimated. It was in the blood.

She was indeed a strange creature, that delicate, dainty, mischievous, tender, God-fearing, inexplicable Southern girl. With her fine grain, her silken hair, her satiny skin, her musical speech; pleasure-loving, saucy, bewitching — deep down lay the bedrock foundation of innate virtue, piety, and womanliness, on which were planted all for which human nature can hope, and all to which it can aspire. Words fail to convey an idea of what she was; as well try to describe the beauty of the rose or the perfume of the violet. To appreciate her one must have seen her, have known her, have loved her.

There are certain other characters

without mention of which no picture of
the social life of the South would be
complete : the old mammies and family
servants about the house. These were
important, and helped to make the life.
The Mammy was the zealous, faithful,
and efficient assistant of the mistress in
all that pertained to the care and training of the children. Her authority was
recognized in all that related to them
directly or indirectly, second only to
that of the Mistress and Master. She
tended them, regulated them, disciplined
them : having authority indeed in cases
to administer correction ; for her affection was undoubted. Her *régime* ex-
tended frequently through two generations, occasionally through three. From
their infancy she was the careful and
faithful nurse, the affection between her
and the children she nursed being often
more marked than that between her
and her own offspring. She may have
been harsh to the latter ; she was never
anything but tender with the others.

Her authority was, in a measure, recognized through life, for her devotion was unquestionable. The young masters and mistresses were her "children" long after they had children of their own. When they parted from her or met with her again after separation, they embraced her with the same affection as when in childhood she "led them smiling into sleep." She was worthy of the affection. At all times she was their faithful ally and champion, excusing them, shielding them, petting them, aiding them, yet holding them up too to a certain high accountability. Her influence was always for good. She received, as she gave, an unqualified affection. If she was a slave, she at least was not a servant, but was an honored member of the family, universally beloved, universally cared for — "the Mammy."

Next to her in importance and rank were the Butler and the Carriage-driver, These with the Mammy were the aristocrats of the family, who trained the

*" She was never anything but tender with the others."*

children in good manners and other exercises ; and uncompromising aristocrats they were. The Butler was apt to be severe, and was feared ; the Driver was genial and kindly, and was adored. I recall a butler, "Uncle Tom," an austere gentleman, who was the terror of the juniors of the connection. One of the children, after watching him furtively as he moved about with grand air, when he had left the room and his footsteps had died away, crept over and asked her grandmother, his mistress, in an awed whisper, "Grandma, are you 'fraid of Unc' Tom ?"

The Driver was the ally of the boys, the worshipper of the girls, and consequently had an ally in their mother, the mistress. As the head of the stable, he was an important personage. This comradeship was never forgotten ; it lasted through life. The years might grow on him, his eyes might become dim ; but he was left in command even when he was too feeble to hold the horses; and though he might no longer grasp the reins, he at least held the title, and to the end was always "the Driver of Mistiss's carriage."

Other servants too there were with special places and privileges,—gardeners and "boys about the house," comrades of the boys; and "own maids," for each girl had her "own maid." They all formed one great family in the social structure now passed away, a structure incredible by those who knew it not, and now, under new conditions, almost incredible by those who knew it best.

The social life formed of these elements combined was one of singular sweetness and freedom from vice. If it was not filled with excitement, it was replete with happiness and content. It is asserted that it was narrow. Perhaps it was. It was so sweet, so charming, that it is little wonder if it asked nothing more than to be let alone.

They who lived it were a careless

*" The Butler was apt to be severe, and was feared."*

and pleasure-loving people; but, as in most rural communities, their festivities were free from dissipation. There was sometimes too great an indulgence on the part of young men in the State drink, the julep; but whether it was that it killed early, or that it was usually abandoned as the responsibilities of life increased, an elderly man of dissipated habits was almost unknown. They were fond of sport, and excelled in it, being generally fine riders, good shots, and skilled hunters. Love of horses was a race characteristic, and fine horsemanship was a thing little considered only because it was universal.

The life was gay. In addition to the perpetual round of ordinary entertainment, there was always on hand or in prospect some more formal festivity, — a club meeting, a fox-hunt, a party, a tournament, a wedding. Little excuse was needed to bring people together where every one was social, and where the great honor was to be the host.

Scientific horse-racing was confined to
the regular race-tracks, where the races
were not dashes, but four-mile heats
which tested speed and bottom alike.
But good blood was common, and
even a ride with a girl in an after-
noon meant generally a dash along the
level through the woods, where, truth
to tell, Miss Atalanta was very apt to
win. Occasionally there was even a
dash from the church. The high-
swung carriages, having received their
precious loads of lily-fingered, pink-
faced, laughing girls with teeth like
pearls and eyes like stars, helped in by
young men who would have thrown not
only their cloaks but their hearts into
the mud to keep those dainty feet from
being soiled, would go ahead; and then,
the restive saddle-horses being untied
from the swinging limbs, the young
gallants would mount, and, by an instinctive common impulse, starting all
together, would make a dash to the
first hill, on top of which the dust still

*The Lady and the Ox-Cart.*

lingered, a golden nimbus thrown from
the wheels that rolled their goddesses.

The chief sport, however, was fox-
hunting. It was, in season, almost
universal. Who that lived in that time
does not remember the fox-hunts, — the
eager chase after "grays" or "old
reds"! The grays furnished more fun,
the reds more excitement. The grays
did not run so far, but usually kept near
home, going in a circuit of six or eight
miles. "An old red," generally so
called irrespective of age, as a tribute to
his prowess, might lead the dogs all day,
and end by losing them as evening
fell, after taking them a dead stretch
for thirty miles. The capture of a gray
was what men boasted of; a chase
after "an old red" was what they
"yarned" about. Some old reds became historical characters, and were as
well known and as much discussed in the
counties they inhabited as the leaders of
the bar or the crack speakers of the
circuit. The wiles and guiles of each

veteran were the pride of his neighbors
and hunters. Many of them had names.
Gentlemen discussed them at their club
dinners; lawyers told stories about
them in the " Lawyers' Rooms " at the
court-houses; young men, while they
waited for the preacher to get well into
the service before going into church,
bragged about them in the churchyards
on Sundays. There was one such that
I remember: he was known as " Nat
Turner," after the notorious leader of
" Nat Turner's Rebellion," who re-
mained in hiding for weeks after all
his followers were taken.

Great frolics these hunts were; for
there were the prettiest girls in the
world in the country houses round
about, and each young fellow was sure
to have in his heart some brown or
blue-eyed maiden to whom he had
promised the brush, and to whom, with
feigned indifference but with mantling
cheek and beating heart, he would carry
it if, as he counted on doing, he should

win it. Sometimes the girls came over themselves and rode, or more likely were already there visiting, and the beaux simply followed them by a law as immutable as that by which the result follows the premises in a mathematical proposition.

Even the boys had their lady-loves, and rode for them on the colts or mules: not the small girls of their own age (no " little girls " for them !). Their sweethearts were grown young ladies, with smiling eyes and silken hair and graceful mien, whom their grown cousins courted, and whom they with their boys' hearts worshipped. Often a half-dozen were in love with one — always the prettiest one — and, with the generous spirit of boys in whom the selfish instinct has not yet awakened, agreed among themselves that they would all ride for her, and that whichever got the brush should present it on behalf of all.

What a gallant sight it was ! The appearance of the hunters on the far hill, in the evening, with their packs surrounding them! Who does not recall the excitement at the house; the arrival in the yard, with horns blowing, hounds baying, horses prancing, and girls laughing; the picture of the young ladies on the front portico with their arms round each other's dainty waists, — the slender, pretty figures, the bright faces, the sparkling eyes, the gay laughter and musical voices, as with coquettish merriment they challenged the riders, demanding to blow the horns themselves or to ride some specially handsome horse next morning! The way, the challenge being accepted, they tripped down the steps, — some with little screams shrinking from the bounding dogs; one or two with stouter hearts, fixed upon higher game, bravely ignoring them and leaving their management to their masters, who at their approach sprang to the ground to meet them, hat in hand and the telltale blood mounting

*An Old-fashioned Grist-Mill.*

to their sunburned faces, handsome with the beauty and pride of youth!

I am painfully aware of the inadequacy of my picture. But who could do justice to the truth!

It was owing to all these and some other characteristics that the life was what it was. It was on a charming key. It possessed an ampleness and generosity which were not splendid because they were too genuine and refined.

Hospitality had become a recognized race characteristic, and was practised as a matter of course. It was universal; it was spontaneous. It was one of the distinguishing features of the civilization; as much a part of the social life as any other of the domestic relations. Its generosity secured it a distinctive title. The exactions it entailed were engrossing. Its exercise occupied much of the time, and exhausted much of the means. The constant intercourse of the neighborhood, with its perpetual

round of dinners, teas, and entertain-
ments, was supplemented by visits of
friends and relatives from other sections,
who came with their families, their
equipages, and personal servants, to
spend a month or two, or as long a
time as they pleased. A dinner invita-
tion was not so designated. It was,
with more exactitude, termed " spend-
ing the day." On Sundays every one
invited every one else from church, and
there would be long lines of carriages
passing in at the open gates.

It is a mystery how the house ever
held the visitors. Only the mistress
knew. Her resources were enormous.
The rooms, with their low ceilings,
were wide, and had a holding capacity
which was simply astounding. The
walls seemed to be made of india-rubber,
so great was their stretching power.
No one who came, whether friend or
stranger, was ever turned away. If the
beds were full — as when were they
not ! — pallets were put down on the

floor in the parlor or the garret for the younger members of the family, sometimes even the passages being utilized. Frequently at Christmas the master and mistress were compelled to resort to the same refuge.

It was this intercourse, following the intermarriage and class feeling of the old families, which made Virginians clannish, and caused a single distinguishable common strain of blood, however distant, to be recognized and counted as kinship.

Perhaps this universal entertainment might not now be considered elegant. Let us see.

It was based upon a sentiment as pure and unselfish as can animate the human mind, — upon kindness. It was easy, generous, and refined. The manners of entertainers and entertained alike were gentle, cordial, simple, with, to strangers, a slight trace of stateliness. The best the hosts had was given; no more was required.

# Social Life

The conversation was surprising; it was of the crops, the roads, history, literature, politics, mutual friends, including the . entire field of neighborhood matters, related not as gossip, but as affairs of common interest, which every one knew or was expected and entitled to know.

Among the ladies, the fashions came in, of course, embracing particularly " patterns."

Politics took the place of honor among the gentlemen, their range embracing not only State and national politics, but British as well, as to which they possessed astonishing knowledge, interest in English matters having been handed down from father to son as a class test. " My father's " opinion was quoted as conclusive authority on this and all points, and in matters of great importance historically " my grandfather, sir," was cited. The peculiarity of the whole was that it was cast on a high plane, and possessed a literary flavor of a high order; for, as has been said, the classics, Latin and English, with a fair sprinkling of good old French authors, were in the bookcases, and were there not for show, but for companionship. There was nothing for show in that life; it was all genuine, real, true.

They had preserved the old customs that their fathers had brought with them from the mother country. The great fête of the people was Christmas. Spring had its special delights, — horse - back rides through the budding

*A Colonial Stove.*

woods, with the birds singing; fishing parties down on the little rivers, with out-of-doors lunches and love-making; parties of various kinds from house to house. Summer had its pleasures, — handsome dinners, and teas with moonlight strolls and rides to follow; visits to or from relatives, or even to the White Sulphur Springs, called simply " the White." The Fall had its pleasures. But all times and seasons paled and dimmed before the festive joys of Christmas. It had been handed down for generations; it belonged to the race. It had come over with their forefathers. It had a peculiar significance. It was a title. Religion had given it its benediction. It was the time to "Shout the glad tidings." It was The Holidays. There were other holidays for the slaves, both of the school-room and the plantation, such as Easter and Whit-Monday; but Christmas was distinctively " The Holidays." Then the boys came home from school or college with their friends; the members of the family who had moved away returned; pretty cousins came for the festivities; the neighborhood grew merry. The

negroes were all to have holiday, the
house-servants taking turn and turn
about, and the plantation, long before
the time, made ready for Christmas
cheer. It was by all the younger
population looked back to half the
year, looked forward to the other
half. Time was measured by it: it
was either so long " since Christmas,"
or so long " before Christmas." The
affairs of the plantation were set in
order against it. The corn was got in;
the hogs were killed; the lard " tried;"
sausage-meat made; mince-meat prepared; turkeys fattened, with " the
big gobbler" specially devoted to the
" Christmas dinner;" the servants'
winter clothes and new shoes stored
away ready for distribution; and the
plantation began to be ready to prepare
for Christmas.

In the first place, there was generally
a cold spell which froze up everything
and enabled the ice-houses to be filled.
(The seasons, like a good many other

things, appear to have changed since that old time before the war.) This spell was the harbinger; and great fun it was at the ice-pond, where the big rafts of ice were floated along, with the boys on them. The rusty skates with their curled runners and stiff straps were gotten out, and maybe tried for a day. Then the stir began. The wagons all were put to hauling wood — hickory. Nothing but hickory now; other wood might do for other times. But at Christmas only hickory was used; and the wood-pile was heaped high with the logs; while to the ordinary wood-cutters " for the house " were added three, four, a half-dozen more, whose shining axes rang around the wood-pile all day long. With what a vim they cut, and how telling was that earnest " Ha'nh! " as they drove the ringing axes into the hard wood, sending the big white chips flying in all directions! It was always the envy of the boys, that simultaneous, ostentatious expulsion of the breath, and they used to try vainly to imitate it.

In the midst of it all came the wagon or the ox-cart from " the depot," with the big white boxes of Christmas things, the black driver feigning hypocritical indifference as he drove through the choppers to the storeroom. Then came the rush of all the cutters to help him unload; the jokes among themselves, as they pretended to strain in lifting, of what " master " or " mistis " was going to give them out of those boxes, uttered just loud enough to reach their master's or mistress's ears where they stood looking on, whilst the driver took due advantage of his temporary prestige to give many pompous cautions and directions.

The getting the evergreens and mistletoe was the sign that Christmas had come, was really here. There were the parlor and hall and dining-room to be " dressed," and, above all, the old church. The last was the work of the neighborhood; all united in it, and it was one of the events of the year. Young men rode thirty and forty miles to "help" dress that church. They did not go home again till after Christmas.

The return from the church was the beginning of the festivities.

Then by "Christmas Eve's eve" the wood was all cut and stacked high in the wood-house and on and under the back porticos, so as to be handy, and secure from the snow which was almost certain to come. It seems that Christmas was almost sure to bring it in old times; at least it is closely associated with it. The excitement increased; the boxes were unpacked, some of them openly, to the general delight; others with a mysterious secrecy which stimulated curiosity to its highest point and added immeasurably to the charm of the occasion. The kitchen filled up with assistants famed for special skill in particular branches of the cook's art, who bustled about with glistening faces

*Dressing the Church.*

and shining teeth, proud of their elevation and eager to prove their merits and add to the general cheer.

It was now Christmas Eve. From time to time the " hired out " servants came home from Richmond or other places where they had been hired or had hired out themselves, their terms having been by common custom framed, with due regard to their rights to the holiday, to expire in time for them to spend the Christmas at home.[1]   There was much hilarity over their arrival, and they were welcomed like members of the family as, with their new winter clothes donned a little ahead of time, they came to pay "bespec's to master and mistis."

Then the vehicles went off to the distant station for the visitors — the visitors and the boys. Oh the excitement of that! at first the drag of the long hours, and then the eager expectancy as the time approached for their return; the

[1] The hiring contracts ran from New Year to Christmas.

" making up " of the fires in the visitors'
rooms (of the big fires; there had been
fires there all day " to air " them, but
now they must be made up afresh);
the hurrying backwards and forwards
of the servants; the feverish impatience
of every one, especially of the children,
who are sure the train is " late " or
that something has " happened," and
who run and look up towards the big
gate every five minutes, notwithstand-
ing the mammy's oft-repeated caution
that a " watch' pot never b'iles."
There was one exception to the general excitement: the Mistress, calm,
deliberate, unperturbed, moved about
with her usual serene composure, her
watchful eye seeing that everything
was " ready." Her orders had been
given and her arrangements made
days before, such was her system.
The young ladies, having finished
dressing the parlor and hall, had dis-
appeared. Satisfied at last with their
work, after innumerable final touches,

every one of which was an undeniable improvement to that which had already appeared perfect, they had suddenly vanished — vanished as completely as a dream — to appear again later on at the parlor door, radiant visions of loveliness, or, maybe, if certain visitors unexpectedly arrived, to meet accidentally in the less embarrassing and safer precincts of the dimly lighted halls or passages. When they appeared, what a transformation had taken place! If they were bewitching before, now they were entrancing. The gay, laughing, saucy creature who had been dressing the parlors and hanging the mistletoe with many jests and parries of the half-veiled references was now a demure or stately maiden in all the dignity of a new gown and with all the graciousness of a young countess.

But this is after the carriages return. They have not yet arrived. They are late — they are always late — and it is dark before they come; the glow of the fires and candles shines out through the windows on the snow, often blackened by the shadows of little figures whose noses are pressed to the cold panes, which grow blurred with their warm breath. Meantime the carriages, piled outside and in, are slowly making their way homeward through the frozen roads, followed by the creaking wagon filled with trunks, on which are haply perched small muffled figures, whose places in the carriages are taken by unexpected guests. The drivers still keep up a running fire with their young masters, though they have long since been pumped dry as to every conceivable matter connected with " home," in return for which they receive information as to school and college pranks. At last the " big gate " is reached; a half-frozen figure rolls out and runs to open it, flapping his arms in the darkness like some strange, uncanny bird; they pass through; the gleam of a light shines away off on a far hill. The

"At last the 'big gate' is reached."

shout goes up, " There she is; I see
her!" The light is lost, but a little
later appears again. It is the light in
the mother's chamber, the curtains of
the windows of which have been left up
intentionally, that the welcoming gleam
may be seen afar off by her boys on the
first hill — a blessed beacon shining
from home and her mother's heart.

Across the white fields the dark
vehicles move, then toil up the house
hill, filled with their eager occupants,
who can scarce restrain themselves;
approach the house, by this time glow-
ing with lighted windows, and enter
the yard just as the doors open and a
swarm rushes out with joyful cries of,
" Here they are!" "Yes, here we
are!" comes in cheery answer, and
one after another they roll or step out,
according to age and dignity, and run
up the steps, stamping their feet, the
boys to be taken fast into motherly
arms, and the visitors to be given
warm handclasps and cordial welcomes.

# Social Life

Later on the children were got to bed, scarce able to keep in their pallets for excitement; the stockings were all hung up over the big fireplace; and the grown people grew gay in the crowded parlors. There was no splendor, nor show, nor style as it would be understood now. Had there been, it could not have been so charming. There were only profusion and sincerity, heartiness and gayety, cordiality and cheer, and withal genuineness and refinement.

Next morning the stir began before light. White-clad little figures stole about in the gloom, with bulging stockings clasped to their bosoms, opening doors, shouting " Christmas gift! " into dark rooms at sleeping elders, and then scurrying away like so many white mice, squeaking with delight, to rake open the embers and inspect their treasures. At prayers, " Shout the glad tidings " was sung by fresh young voices with due fervor.

How gay the scene was at breakfast! What pranks had been performed in the name of Santa Claus! Every foible had been played on. What lovely telltale blushes and glances and laughter greeted the confessions! The larger part of the day was spent in going to and coming from the beautifully dressed church, where the service was read, and the anthems and hymns were sung by every one, for every one was happy.

But, as in the beginning of things, "the evening and the morning were the first day." Dinner was the great event. It was the test of the mistress and the cook, or, rather, the cooks; for the kitchen now was full of them. It is impossible to describe it. The old mahogany table, stretched diagonally across the dining-room, groaned; the big gobbler filled the place of honor; a great round of beef held the second place; an old ham, with every other dish that ingenuity, backed by long

95

experience, could devise, was at the side, and the shining sideboard, gleaming with glass, scarcely held the dessert. The butler and his assistants were supernaturally serious and slow, which bespoke plainly too frequent a recourse to the apple-toddy bowl; but under the stimulus of the mistress's eye, they got through all right, and their slight unsteadiness was overlooked.

It was then that the fun began.

After dinner there were apple-toddy and egg-nog, as there had been before.

There were games and dances — country dances, the lancers and quadrilles. The top of the old piano was lifted up, and the infectious dancing-tunes rolled out under the flying fingers. Haply there was some demur on the part of the elder ladies, who were not quite sure that it was right; but it was overruled by the gentlemen, and the master in his frock coat and high collar started the ball by catching the prettiest girl by the hand and leading her to the

*The Virginia Reel.*

head of the room right under the noses of half a dozen bashful lovers, calling to them meantime to " get their sweethearts and come along." Round dancing was not yet introduced. It was regarded as an innovation, if nothing worse. It was held generally as highly improper, by some as " disgusting." As to the german, why, had it been known, the very name would have been sufficient to damn it. Nothing foreign in that civilization! There was fun enough in the old-fashioned country dances, and the " Virginia reel " at the close. Whoever could not be satisfied with that was hard to please.

But it was not only in the " great house " that there was Christmas cheer. Every cabin was full of it, and in the wash-house or the carpenter-shop there was preparation for a plantation supper.

At this time, too, there were the negro parties, where the ladies and gentlemen went to look on, the sup-

per having been superintended by the
mistresses, and the tables being deco-
rated by their own white hands.
There was almost sure to be a negro
wedding during the holidays. The
ceremony might be performed in the
dining-room or in the hall by the
master, or in one of the quarters by a
colored preacher ; but it was a gay occasion, and the dusky bride's trousseau
had been arranged by her young mistress, and the family was on hand to
get fun out of the entertainment, and
to recognize by their presence the
solemnity of the tie.

Other weddings there were, too,
sometimes following these Christmas
gayeties, and sometimes occurring " just
so," because the girls were the loveliest
in the world, and the men were lovers
almost from their boyhood. How
beautiful our mothers must have been
in their youth to have been so beautiful
in their age !

There were no long journeys for the

*A Negro Wedding.*

young married folk in those times; the travelling was usually done before marriage. When a wedding took place, however, the entire neighborhood entertained the young couple.

Truly it was a charming life. There was a vast waste; but it was not loss. Every one had food, every one had raiment, every one had peace. There was not wealth in the base sense in which we know it and strive for it and trample down others for it now. But there was wealth in the good old sense in which the litany of our fathers used it. There was weal. There was the best of all wealth; there was content, and "a quiet mind is richer than a crown."

We have gained something by the change. The South under her new conditions will in time grow rich, will wax fat; nevertheless we have lost much. How much only those who knew it can estimate; to them it was inestimable.

# Social Life

That the social life of the Old South had its faults I am far from denying. What civilization has not? But its virtues far outweighed them; its graces were never equalled. For all its faults, it was, I believe, the purest, sweetest life ever lived. It has been claimed that it was non-productive, that it fostered sterility. Only ignorance or folly could make the assertion. It largely contributed to produce this nation; it led its armies and its navies; it established this government so firmly that not even it could overthrow it; it opened up the great West; it added Louisiana and Texas, and more than trebled our territory; it christianized the negro race in a little over two centuries, impressed upon it regard for order, and gave it the only civilization it has ever possessed since the dawn of history. It has maintained the supremacy of the Caucasian race, upon which all civilization seems now to depend. It produced a people whose heroic fight

*A Typical Negro Cabin.*

against the forces of the world has enriched the annals of the human race, —
a people whose fortitude in defeat has been even more splendid than their valor in war. It made men noble, gentle, and brave, and women tender and pure and true. It may have fallen short in material development in its narrower sense, but it abounded in spiritual development; it made the domestic virtues as common as light and air, and filled homes with purity and peace.

It has passed from the earth, but it has left its benignant influence behind it to sweeten and sustain its children. The ivory palaces have been destroyed, but myrrh, aloes, and cassia still breathe amid their dismantled ruins.